Make Your Own Weather Station

by Melvin Berger

illustrated by Mark Teague

SCHOLASTIC INC.
New York Toronto London Auckland Sydney

Photo Credits

Page 4: Leo de Wys. Page 5: Photo Researchers.
Page 6: Photo Researchers. Page 9: Photo take;
Gene Moore. Page 18: Leo de Wys; Everett Johnson.

ISBN 0-590-43877-8

Copyright © 1991 by Melvin Berger.

Illustrations copyright © 1991 by Scholastic Inc.

All rights reserved. Published by Scholastic Inc., 730 Broadway, New York, NY 10003.

12 11 10 9 8 7 6 5 4 3 2 1   1 2 3 4 5 6/9

Printed in the U.S.A.   33

First Scholastic printing, September 1991

CONTENTS

Weather satellite

Meteorologist at work

Become a Weather Watcher

The modern weather stations of the National Weather Service are amazing places. They are run by scientists called meteorologists.

Meteorologists use many special and complex electronic instruments in their work. Satellites track the world's weather from hundreds of miles up in space. Giant weather balloons measure conditions in the earth's atmosphere. High-speed computers then bring all this information together. They help the scientists make their forecasts.

But the meteorologists of the National Weather Service are not the only people keeping track of the weather. Many people all over our country enjoy weather watching as a hobby, using their eyes and simple instruments to forecast weather conditions.

This book can help you become a top-notch weather watcher, too. It tells you how to:

- use the weather instruments that come with this book.
- make your own weather instruments.
- keep track of the weather on your own weather chart.
- forecast local weather conditions.

Your observations may help the meteorologists at the National Weather Service. Sometimes they need to know the temperature, the amount of rain or snow, or the wind speed and direction at different places around the country.

But you can discover even more about weather conditions where you live. You can:

- keep track of rising or falling air pressure.
- measure the humidity in the air.
- find the windchill factor.
- identify different types of clouds.
- test for smoke and particle pollution.

You're sure to enjoy having your own weather station. Weather watching can be lots of fun. It may even lead, one day, to a career as a meteorologist!

Weather balloon

Instrument Shelter

All weather watchers need an instrument shelter. The shelter protects your instruments. But at the same time it must be open to the weather.

You can make your instrument shelter out of a large cardboard carton.

Materials you need:

a cardboard carton
two large brads
a rubber band
waterproof paint
rocks

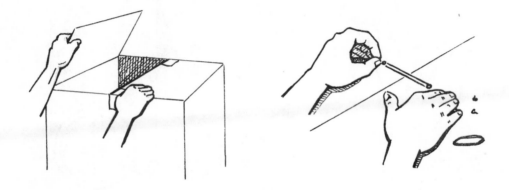

Get a big, clean, dry box that has either a single top or four flaps on top. The best ones are found in liquor stores or supermarkets.

A carton with its top in one piece is ideal. The top lifts up and makes a door to the shelter.

If your carton has four flaps, ask an adult to cut off the two shorter flaps. Then fold one long flap over so that it covers part of the opening. Tape that flap into place. Leave the other flap free to open and close.

Make a latch for your door with two large brads and a rubber band.

Use one brad to hold the rubber band in place on the top flap or on the top edge of your box. Insert the second brad into the bottom flap so that you can latch your door shut by pulling the rubber band down around the head of the brad.

Next, you want to protect your instrument shelter from the rain and snow. An easy way is to paint it all over—inside and out—with waterproof paint. You may want to use bright colors and decorate it with designs or pictures.

Find a spot outdoors to place your instrument shelter. The shelter works best if it is about four feet above the ground and quite far from any building or wall.

Go to the spot with the compass in this book. Hold the compass flat in your hand. Wait a minute until the needle stops jiggling around.

Look closely at the needle. You'll see that one end is colored blue. That end points north. The compass card under the needle may have north pointing in a different direction. But the blue end of the needle always points north.

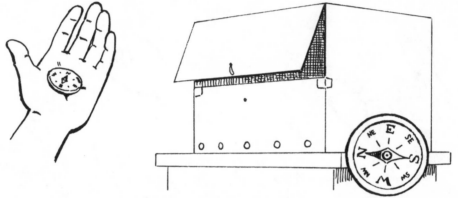

Set the shelter on a table or stand of some sort. Place it so that the opening faces north. Be sure that the flap—whether a whole side or only half a side—swings up. That will let you reach inside the shelter easily.

Put a few heavy rocks inside the shelter. That will keep the shelter from blowing away on a windy or stormy day.

Finally, poke several small holes into each side of the box. This will let air flow through the shelter.

What if you don't have an outdoor spot for your instrument shelter? Perhaps your teacher will help you find a place in the school yard. If you live in an apartment house, maybe you can put it on a terrace or on the roof. Sometimes a friend will let you set your instrument shelter in the backyard of his or her house. If all else fails, you can keep the shelter indoors and make some—but not all—kinds of observations.

Barometer

The most important tool for forecasting the weather is the barometer. The barometer measures air pressure. Knowing the air pressure helps meteorologists to predict the weather.

One kind of barometer is called an altimeter.

Air pressure is a measure of the weight of the air. It is always changing. When air is cold and dry it weighs the most. Then the barometer shows high or rising air pressure. That tells the meteorologist that fair weather is on its way.

Air that is warm and damp weighs less than dry air. Then the barometer shows low or falling air pressure. A drop in air pressure usually signals foul weather ahead.

Meteorologists use instruments especially made to measure barometric pressure. But you can make a simple barometer from materials you have around the house.

Materials you need:

a clean, dry, quart-sized mayonnaise jar
a large balloon (use the one that comes with this book)
a plastic drinking straw
a strong rubber band
a toothpick

Now you're ready to make and use your barometer:

1. Cut the neck off the balloon and stretch the balloon over the mouth of the jar.

2. Place the rubber band around the neck of the jar to hold the balloon in place.

3. Cut one end of the drinking straw to a point. Tape the other end of the straw horizontally to the center of the balloon.

4. Glue the toothpick to the balloon along the edge of the mouth of the jar, underneath the straw.

5. Stand your barometer in the shelter so that the straw points to a side wall of the shelter.

6. Draw a line on the shelter wall at the same level as the straw. Or, tape a piece of paper to the wall and draw the line on the paper. Mark today's date next to the line.

7. Check the pointer level each day at about the same time. And each day draw a new line and note the date. If the new line is higher, the pressure is rising. If the new line is lower, the pressure is falling. If the lines stay about the same, the pressure is steady and not changing.

8. Notice if the pressure is rising, falling, or steady day by day.

Here's why the level of the pointer of your barometer changes. By stretching the balloon over the mouth of the jar, you've sealed the air inside. When the outside air is cold and dry it presses down very hard on the balloon. It squeezes the inside air. The balloon sinks down. And the straw points a little higher.

When the outside air is warm and damp, it doesn't press as hard. The air in the jar is able to spread out or expand. This moves the balloon up a bit. And the straw points a little lower.

Remember:

- A rising barometer usually means fair weather.
- A falling barometer usually means foul weather.
- A steady barometer usually means no change in the weather.

Thermometer

Air is sometimes hot. Sometimes it is cold. We measure the temperature of the air with a thermometer.

The air that surrounds the earth is warmed by the sun. That's why the air is usually warmer during the day—when the sun is shining—than at night.

In the summertime, the sun's rays shine more directly on the earth than during the winter. Also, on summer days the sun shines for more hours than on winter days. This makes summer temperatures higher than winter temperatures.

Look at the thermometer that comes with this book. Do you see the red liquid in the round bulb at the bottom of the glass tube?

As the air becomes hot, the liquid grows bigger, or expands. It needs more room. Where can it go? The only place is up the tube.

When the air becomes cold, the liquid cools off. It takes less room. Down the tube it slides.

Lines on the thermometer show the temperature in degrees (°). Marked on one side is the Fahrenheit or F scale. On the other side is the Celsius or C scale.

The F scale has 180 divisions between the freezing point of water (32° F) and the boiling point of water (212° F).

The Celsius or C scale has 100 divisions between the freezing point of water (0° C) and the boiling point of water (100° C). This scale is the one most used by meteorologists.

Now get ready to put your thermometer to work:

1. Stand the thermometer inside your instrument shelter. By keeping the thermometer in the shade you measure the air temperature, not the heat of the sun.

2. Do not touch the bulb with your hand. Your hand is warm and will raise the temperature.

3. To follow daily changes in the temperature, read your thermometer at the same time every day—morning, afternoon, or evening. And always read the same scale, either F or C. Which month has the highest temperatures? Which month has the lowest readings?

4. To follow temperature changes during one day, read your thermometer every hour. What time of the day is coldest? What time is warmest?

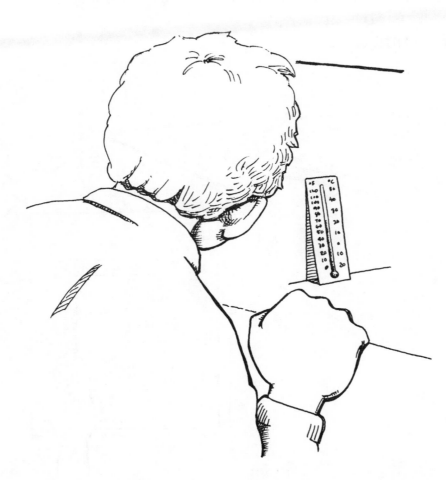

Hygrometer

Air always contains a certain amount of water. The water comes from the evaporation of the world's oceans, lakes, and rivers. Evaporation changes water from a liquid into a gas. The gas is called water vapor. Water vapor is invisible. It disappears into the air.

Sometimes there's a lot of water vapor in the air. The air feels damp and sticky. We say there is high humidity. Other times, there is little water vapor in the air. We say the air is dry or has low humidity.

You can make your own hygrometer. It will give you a measure of the amount of humidity in the air. It will tell you whether there is high or low humidity.

Materials you need:

a piece of heavy cardboard about 9″ × 12″
one long human hair about 9″ (If you don't have long hair, ask a friend with long hair to save you a strand from her brush or comb.)
two thumbtacks

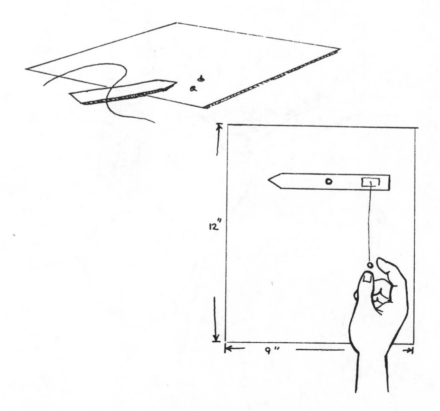

14

1. Wash the strand of hair in hot soapy water and let it dry.

2. Punch out the pointer from the center of the book.

3. Use a sharp pencil, pen, or pin to poke out the two holes in the pointer.

4. Thread one end of the hair through the hole that is nearer the blunt end of the pointer. Use a small piece of tape to attach the hair to the pointer.

5. Set the pointer down on the cardboard. Place it about 3 inches below the top 9″ edge of the cardboard. The pointer should be about 2 inches from the left 12″ edge. Attach the pointer loosely to the cardboard. Do this by pushing a thumbtack through the second hole and into the cardboard. Wiggle the pointer up and down to make sure it can move freely.

6. Push another thumbtack partway into the cardboard. The thumbtack should be about 6 inches below the spot where the hair is attached to the pointer.

7. Gently pull and stretch the hair down and wrap it around this thumbtack.

8. Now push this thumbtack tightly into the cardboard. The pointer on your hygrometer is now set to show the humidity. When there is a lot of moisture in the air, the hair gets just a little bit longer. That makes the pointer go *lower*. This means *higher* humidity.

   When the air is drier, the hair gets a little bit shorter. Then the pointer goes *higher*. This tells you there is *lower* humidity.

Try it out. Tune your radio or TV to a weather report. (Some all-news radio stations give the weather every 10 minutes or so. Or watch the weather channel on cable TV.) Listen for the relative humidity. The announcer may say, for example: "The relative humidity is sixty percent." That tells you the amount of moisture in the air (60%), compared to how much moisture the air could hold (100%).

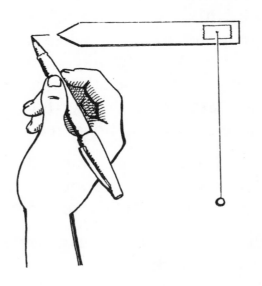

Place your hygrometer in the instrument shelter. Rest it against one of the side walls. Wait half an hour for the hair to stretch or contract. Then draw a line on the wall at the level where the arrow is pointing. Write down the official relative humidity—say 60%—at that point.

The next day, listen again to the radio or TV. Draw a new line and enter the new relative humidity. Do this daily for at least one week.

After a week or more, the numbers on your shelter wall will form a scale. Then you'll be able to tell the relative humidity by looking at the pointer. You won't need to listen to the radio or TV.

Low humidity is 50% or less moisture in the air. High humidity is any amount over 50%. The higher the humidity, the greater the percentage of water in the air.

Wind Gauge

see page 17

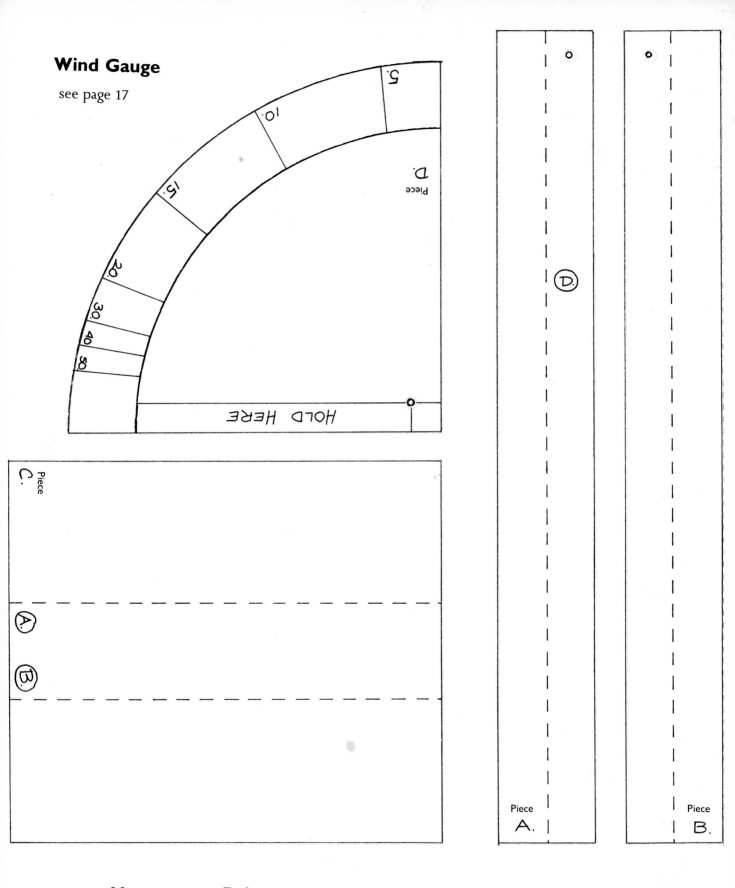

HOLD HERE

Piece D.

5.
10.
15.
20.
30.
40.
50.

Piece C.

A.

B.

Piece A.

Piece B.

D.

Hygrometer Pointer

see page 14

see page 26

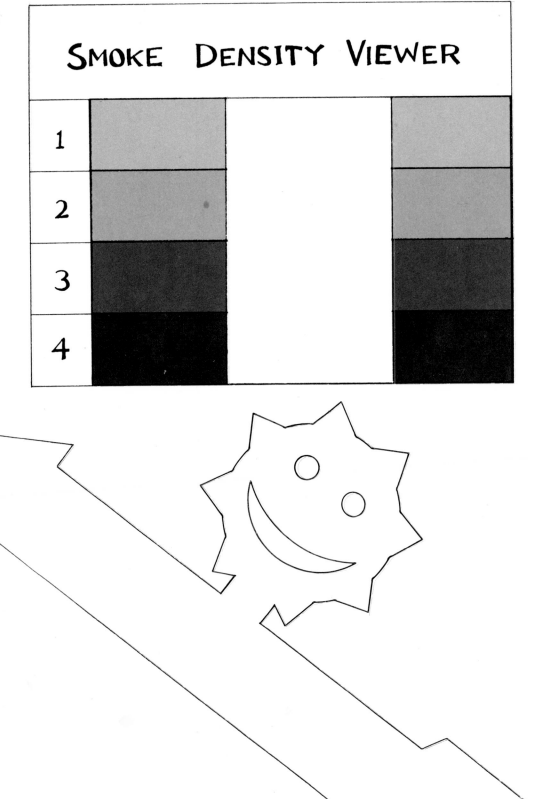

Weather Vane

see page 20

Wind Gauge

When air moves from one place to another it makes a wind. Winds can be created in several ways.

Air can be pushed. When you blow out a candle or turn on a fan you are pushing air.

Changing temperatures also make air move. Air that is warmed becomes lighter. The warm air rises up over the cold air. The rising warm air makes a wind.

In the same way, air that is chilled becomes heavier. It sinks down. As it drops down it makes a wind.

Also, air is pulled from areas of high pressure to areas of low pressure. The air moving from high pressure to low pressure creates a wind.

The wind gauge allows you to make more accurate measurements of wind speed. Put together the wind gauge in the center of this book.

Directions for making the Wind Gauge

1. Punch out all four pieces along the solid lines.

2. Fold pieces A and B up along the dotted lines so that the dotted lines are inside the fold.

3. Match letter A (on piece A) to the circled A (on piece C). Tape the left edge of piece A to piece C along the dotted line.

4. Match letter B (on piece B) to the circled B (on piece C). Tape the right edge of piece B to piece C along the dotted line.

5. Use a sharp pencil to poke out the small holes in pieces A, B, and D.

6. Line up the holes of pieces A, B, and D, with piece D in between pieces A and B. Make sure the "D" on piece D matches the circled D on piece A.

7. Use needle and thread to connect pieces A, B, and D. Your Wind Gauge is now ready.

Take your wind gauge outdoors. Hold it at the place marked on the gauge. Turn yourself around slowly until the wind blows directly on the movable part of the wind gauge.

Now check your wind gauge. How far has it moved? The edge of the movable part shows the approximate wind speed in miles per hour. Record wind speeds on your weather chart.

Using a wind gauge

Beaufort Wind Speed Scale

Many weather watchers use the Beaufort Scale to estimate the speed of the wind. This scale was worked out in 1805 by Sir Francis Beaufort, an admiral in the British Navy. With this scale, you can tell the approximate wind speed based on things you can see and feel.

BEAUFORT SCALE			
Observation	Description	Miles Per Hour	No.
Smoke goes straight up.	Calm	0–1	0
Smoke drifts; weather vane doesn't move.	Light air	1–3	1
Wind felt on face; leaves rustle.	Slight breeze	4–7	2
Leaves and twigs move; bits of paper fly.	Gentle breeze	8–12	3
Small branches sway.	Moderate breeze	13–18	4
Small trees sway; dust clouds rise.	Fresh breeze	19–24	5
Large branches sway; hard to hold umbrellas.	Strong breeze	25–31	6
Large trees sway; hard to walk.	Moderate gale	32–38	7
Twigs break off trees.	Fresh gale	39–46	8
Branches break; some damage to buildings.	Strong gale	47–54	9
Trees blow down; major building damage.	Whole gale	55–63	10
Widespread damage.	Storm	64–75	11
Extreme damage and destruction.	Hurricane	Over 75	12

Weather Vane

Weather vanes show the direction the wind is blowing.

Materials you need:

a cottage-cheese container with lid
a long nail
small stones
an aluminum pie plate
a plastic drinking straw

Here's how to make a weather vane:

1. Paint your clean, dry cottage-cheese container and lid however you wish.

2. Ask a grown-up to poke a long nail up through the center of the container bottom.

3. Ask a grown-up to cut a dime-sized hole in the exact center of the lid with pointed scissors.

4. Put a few small stones inside the container to add weight. Place the stones away from the nail. Set the lid firmly in place on top of the container.

5. Use a pen to write the letter N, for north, at any point near the edge of the lid. Directly under the N, near the opposite side of the lid, mark S, for south. Halfway between the N and the S, on the right-hand side, mark E, for east. And halfway between the N and the S on the left-hand side mark W, for west. Put the container aside.

6. With a pair of scissors, cut out the flat, center part of an aluminum pie plate.

7. Place the flat circle under the design on the center page. Use a ballpoint pen to trace the weather vane design on that page. Press hard so that the pen will mark the aluminum underneath. Cut out the weather vane from the aluminum.

8. Staple the midpoint of the weather vane to one end of a plastic drinking straw.

9. Slip the straw through the hole in the lid of the container and over the nail.

10. Set your compass on top of the instrument shelter. Note which way the blue end of the needle is pointing. That way is north. Put your weather vane on the shelter with the letter N facing in that direction.

As the wind blows, it turns the weather vane. The arrow always points into the wind. That gives you the name of the wind. For example, an arrow pointing to the north tells you it is a north wind. North winds blow from north to south. By noting which way the weather vane is pointing, you know whether it is a north, south, east, or west wind.

Sometimes your weather vane will point between two directions. These directions have special names:

• Between north and east is northeast.

• Between east and south is southeast.

• Between south and west is southwest.

• Between west and north is northwest.

Windchill Factor

A breeze on a warm day makes you feel comfortable. But a wind on a cold day makes you feel even colder. The effect of cold air *plus* wind is called the windchill factor.

This chart will let you determine the windchill factor. The number is based on the temperature and the wind speed in miles per hour.

For example, if your thermometer reads 30°F and your wind gauge reads 15 miles per hour, the windchill factor is 9°F.

Actual Temperature (F)

50° 40° 30° 20° 10° 0° −10° −20° −30° −40°

Windchill Factor

Wind										
Calm	50°	40°	30°	20°	10°	0°	−10°	−20°	−30°	−40°
5 m.p.h.	48°	37°	27°	16°	6°	−5°	−15°	−26°	−36°	−47°
10 m.p.h.	40°	29°	16°	4°	−9°	−21°	−33°	−46°	−58°	−70°
15 m.p.h.	36°	22°	9°	−5°	−18°	−36°	−46°	−58°	−72°	−85°
20 m.p.h.	32°	18°	4°	−10°	−25°	−39°	−53°	−67°	−82°	−96°
25 m.p.h.	30°	16°	0°	−15°	−29°	−44°	−59°	−74°	−88°	−104°
30 m.p.h.	28°	13°	−2°	−18°	−33°	−48°	−63°	−79°	−94°	−109°
35 m.p.h.	27°	11°	−4°	−20°	−35°	−49°	−67°	−82°	−98°	−113°
40 m.p.h.	26°	10°	−6°	−21°	−37°	−53°	−69°	−85°	−100°	−116°

Clouds

Clouds are masses of tiny water drops or ice crystals floating in the air.

Look up at the sky. Do you see any clouds? Match up the clouds in the sky with the cloud pictures on the Weather Poster bound into this book.

Clouds have four basic formations: cumulus, cirrus, stratus, and nimbus. And there are any number of combined cloud formations.

Weather forecasters use cloud formations to help them predict the weather:

Cumulus clouds on a summer morning ▶ afternoon showers or thunderstorms.

Heavy cumulus clouds ▶ squalls or storm.

Line of cumulus clouds ▶ strong winds.

Dark cumulus clouds ▶ hail and strong winds.

Cirrus clouds followed by altostratus clouds ▶ thickening clouds and either rain or snow.

Nimbus or nimbostratus clouds ▶ rain or snow.

Precipitation Gauge

Precipitation is either rain, snow, hail, or sleet that falls to earth. Rain is liquid water. Snow is frozen water vapor that falls as snowflakes. Sleet is frozen rain. And hail is a mixture of either snow or hail and rain.

A precipitation gauge measures the amount of rain, snow, hail, or sleet that has fallen. The amount is usually given in inches or fractions of an inch.

Materials you need:

a clean, empty coffee can and the
plastic lid that comes with it
paint
glue or thumbtacks
a ruler

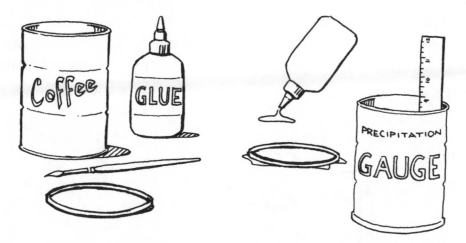

1. Paint the coffee can however you wish.

2. Attach the plastic lid, flat side down, to the top of the shelter. You can use glue or a couple of thumbtacks. Then set the coffee can, with the open end up, firmly into its plastic cap.

Following a heavy rain or snowstorm, you can measure the precipitation. Place the ruler straight down into the can. How high does the precipitation reach?

If there is no heavy storm, leave your precipitation gauge out for a week or a month. Then measure the total precipitation. Some of the water will have evaporated, but you will still get some idea of how much has fallen.

Test for Smoke Pollution

Air that contains large amounts of smoke is polluted. Any power plant, incinerator, factory, truck, or jet plane that sends out clouds of dark smoke pollutes the air.

You can measure the darkness, or density, of smoke with the Smoke Density Viewer on the center page of this book.

Line up the viewer with smoke coming out of a chimney, smokestack, or exhaust pipe. Check the density of the smoke against the scale. Is it pale gray? That's number 1. Is it black? That's number 4. Or is it somewhere in-between? That's either 2 or 3.

If the smoke has a density of 3 or 4, report the information to your local air pollution agency. Be sure your report includes the date, time, and place you saw the smoke. The officials may also want to know the wind speed at the time. (Use your wind gauge.) And they may ask for the wind direction as well. (Use your weather vane.)

Test for Particle Pollution

Particles are tiny bits of matter that float about in the air. Too many particles of dangerous chemicals in the air cause air pollution.

You can count the number of airborne particles inside and outside your home.

Materials you need:

10 index cards
magnifying glass
roll of white masking tape

1. Write the number 1 in one corner of a card.

2. Cut a 4-inch strip from the tape.

3. Fold back the two ends of the tape and attach them to the card so that the sticky side faces out.

4. With another piece of tape, attach the card to the outside of a window.

5. Number the other cards from 2 to 10 and repeat steps 2, 3, and 4. Place these cards inside and outside several different windows in your house. Be sure that some of the windows face in different directions.

6. Make a chart with the following columns: *Card Number, Window Location, Inside or Outside,* and *Window Direction.* (Use your compass to fill in the last column.)

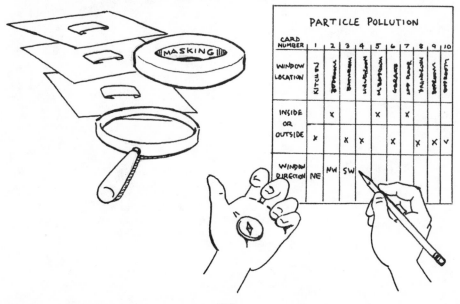

7. After a day or two collect the cards. Any particles that fly by will be caught on the sticky part of the tape.

Look at the sticky part of the tape through the magnifying glass. Do you see the particles that have been trapped there? Do some tapes have more particles than others? Do you see differences between—

- inside and outside cards?
- cards facing different directions?

Can you explain the differences?

Mark off a 1/4-inch square near the center of each piece of tape. With the magnifying glass count the number of particles in the square.

If you find 15 or fewer particles, the air is clean. If there are more than 50 particles, the air is badly polluted.

Weather Chart

Good weather watchers make daily observations and always at the same time of the day. They then enter their findings on a weather chart. You will find a blank weather chart on page 32.

Before starting to fill in your weather chart, it's a good idea to make a few copies. You can either photocopy the chart or copy it over by hand on lined paper.

Make your observations each day. Enter the results in the first blank column.

Here's what you should write:

1. DATE AND HOUR. The exact hour, day, month, and year of your observation.

2. WEATHER CONDITIONS. A single word that best describes the general weather, such as clear, sunny, cloudy, hazy, foggy, rain, snow, hail, or sleet.

3. AIR PRESSURE. The change in air pressure—rising, steady, or falling. Use the barometer.

4. TEMPERATURE. The air temperature in degrees. Use the thermometer.

5. HUMIDITY. The relative humidity. Use the hygrometer.

6. WIND SPEED. How fast the wind is blowing. Use the Beaufort Scale or the wind gauge.

7. WIND DIRECTION. Source of the wind. Use the weather vane or compass.

8. WINDCHILL. The combination of temperature and wind speed in cold weather. Use the Windchill Factor chart.

9. CLOUD TYPE. The cloud formations you see in the sky. Use the Cloud Poster.

10. PRECIPITATION TYPE. The kind of precipitation—rain, snow, hail, or sleet.

11. PRECIPITATION AMOUNT. The quantity of precipitation. Use the precipitation gauge.

12. COMMENTS. Any unusual aspects of the weather. Among the possibilities are smoke or particle pollution, fast changes in weather conditions, sun shower, rainbow, and so on.

The seven blank columns will let you enter all of your observations for a week on a single weather chart. Use copies of the weather chart for future observations.

Weather Forecasting

Predicting the weather is difficult and complex. But a few general rules can be very helpful.

Fair weather is usually coming if:

- the barometer is rising or steady.
- the wind blows from the north or west.
- yesterday's sunset was bright and red.
- any morning fog burns off by noon.
- there are cumulus clouds on a summer afternoon.
- the winds shift clockwise (such as from south to west).

Stormy or rainy weather is usually coming if:

- the barometer is falling.
- the north wind shifts to the east.
- the sky is dark to the west.
- there is a ring around the moon.
- there are clusters of high, wispy cirrus clouds.
- the dawn is bright and red.

The temperature will usually fall if:

- the wind blows from the north or northwest.
- the sky is clear at night and the wind is light.

The temperature will usually rise if:

- the wind is from the south.
- there is a cloud cover at night.

WEATHER CHART

	MONDAY	TUESDAY	WEDNESDAY	THURSDAY	FRIDAY	SATURDAY	SUNDAY
DATE AND HOUR							
WEATHER CON- DITIONS							
AIR PRESSURE							
TEM- PER- ATURE							
HUMIDITY							
WIND SPEED							
WIND DIRECTION							
WIND- CHILL							
CLOUD TYPE							
PRECIP- ITATION TYPE							
PRECIP- ITATION AMOUNT							
COMMENTS							